URBAN TALES OF THE BIBLE SHORT STORY SERIES BOOK 1 - THE PROPHET & THE HO'

Written by T.S. HOLDER
May 8, 2022

The Bible stories and version used in this publication were accessed, respectively, through https://www.biblegateway.com and "Scripture taken from *The Message*. Copyright © 1993, 1994, 1995, 1996, 2000, 2001, 2002. Used by permission of NavPress Publishing Group."

Printed in the United States of America

ISBN 9798-9854404-3-0

This book series is dedicated to all of the elders in my family line. Those that have gone before us and those that are still here. Thank you for leaving a strong and powerful legacy of loving Yeshua.

If you would like TS Holder to do a live reading and/or for autographed copies email TS Holder at Suprnatrl@gmail.com and put TS Holder - Live Reading or TS Holder - Autographed Copies in the subject line.

Introduction

If you were to perform a search on YouTube, Google, and Yahoo or even go to certain pages of Facebook you will find that there are many modern day true stories that will pop-up in the search results similar to this one, but with one exception did God say do it?

There have been so many men and women of God, Pastors, Preachers, Prophets, Evangelists, Teachers, Bishops and Archbishops (did I get them all?) that have been caught up in the trap on both sides of the coin, due to their own inability to control their sexual appetites, but in this case God told Hosea to go out and get himself a street walkin' ho' and marry her. Can you imagine what Hosea was thinking when he received this Word from God! WOW!

Might I add a quick note here, prophets of old were of a much different cloth and caliber than many of the modern day prophets. Prophets of old had a standard of accuracy and truth. There was a strong element of quality control. If the prophets of the Bible missed the mark on their prophetic words it could certainly mean "DEATH." Accuracy was job one!!

Today we have witnessed so many unchecked proph-a-liars, who don't seem to be afraid of God's punishment and who have not been held accountable for the lies. Prime example the 2020 Presidential election. How many prophesied that #45 would win again? How many were wrong? How many were held accountable? How many are still holding that #45 is the true president? There were a few who came back and held themselves accountable and publicly repented, but to this day many are still holding on to and saying that they were correct even though their prophetic word bore no fruit!

Well so much for present day drama, let's get right into this interesting sit-chu-mation of a story!

Hosea 1 – Athaliah the Demonic Queen Mother & the Prophet & the Ho

The time of this story takes place when Kings Uzziah, Jothan, Ahaz and Hezekiah were running things. The other king in charge was King Jeroboam who was the son of Joash. To give you a little insight and backstory that brings us to the book of Hosea or as I call it, The Prophet & The Ho, let's consider the book of 2 Kings Chapter 11.

Now, Joash, who was considered the "BOY KING", came from a family of kings who had a generational history of being wicked and evil. Even his grandmother was known to be a wicked, back-biting, scheming, stone cold murderer! Oh yeah, she was sumthin' else!

This witch, named Queen Mother Athaliah, Joash's grandmother, decided that she wanted the throne for herself. She came to this conclusion after her husband and their son died. She was sitting in the royal palace and thought to herself, "What is going to happen to me now that my husband and son are gone? Who will take the throne and what does that mean for me? They will probably put me out of the palace and send me somewhere to live with the regular folks who are so far beneath me that I can't even see them! Naw, I gotta come up with something to set things off and tilt the tide in my direction! The only solution that I can see is if I kill everyone that might even get close to sitting on the throne! I need to make a blood sacrifice to Baal!"

So with that she tried her best to kill off the entire royal family! Yes, Queen Mother was THEE Queen Demon in the flesh and wanted her bloodline dead and offered up to Baal as a sacrifice!!

Side note: I just gotta say this! I see so many people that are so eager to have a spiritual title in front of their name call themselves Queen Mother. After reading this do you really think that Queen Mother is a title to have? Ya might not want to attach that title to your name because there is rule concerning the things of the spirit that says you are also attaching that accompanying murdering, power hungry, blood-thirsty spirit that Queen Mother Athaliah had to your name as well. Be ye so careful of what you are tapping into and conjuring up! I'm just saying, just saying!

Back to the story which I think is worse than any thriller on T.V. Now, if it had not been for Queen Mother's half-sister Jehosheba, Joash would have been murdered right along with the rest of the royal family line! Jehosheba took little baby Joash and his nurse and hid them away and it was because of

Jehosheba and her husband the High Priest Jehoiada, that baby Joash and his nurse were safe for the next six years. Jehosheba said to her husband Jehoiada, the High Priest, "My sister has lost what little bit of mind she has left! I cannot believe that she actually had her entire family, the royal family killed! What kinda demon has taken a hold of her?"

Jehoiada the priest said, "Yes Lord! Your sister is off the chain right now and acting like Queen Demon in the flesh! We gotta do something about her or else she might come for us, especially if she learns that we are keeping baby boy alive."

He continued, "Queen Mother is really somethin' tuther! She just TOOK the throne for herself by killing everyone off. Who does that? Not only did she take the throne for herself but she got rid of anything that was sacred and that resembled God.

Yes ma'am, she took all the sacred items that we used to worship God with and she is now using them to worship her demon god Baal. I hope that God strikes her where she stands! She is an abomination and we must, no we WILL, do something to bring this kingdom back to God! We ain't going out like this!"

Now, the High Priest Jehoiada did come up with a brilliant scheme to get the throne back from this demonic Queen Mother and give it to the rightful king, little Joash and more importantly back to God. Apparently Queen Mother's kingdom popularity ratings were at an all-time low! 99.9% of the people couldn't stand that old bird, so the takeover scheme was relatively easy to carry out. Jehoiada called the Captains of the Royal Army together and said, "Look, we gotta do something about this Queen Mother. She is outta control!"

The captains of the Royal Army said, "Yes, we agree. That demon needs to go down and we don't have a problem doing it!"

Jehoiada said, "That's what I'm talking about! We all agree that she is doing way, way too much. I have a plan, but I will need your help. Can I count on you to do your part and have my back on this? You down?"

The captains all said, "Yes. We gotchu! And better yet, consider the old bird, demon queen GOT!"

Jehoiada said, "Ok, here is the master plan. I will get the other priests to go to the house of worship and bring back the weapons that King David used. They are on display in the house of worship. These weapons have a special anointing on them which gives them power to overcome evil and we are surely dealing with the highest level of evil, wouldn't you agree?"

The captains all nodded their heads in agreeance and said, "Yes, this is the worst kind of evil. A murdering high ranking demon with that takeover spirit."

Then Jehoiada said, "I need you to swear to me on yo mama's life that you will not tell anyone that does not need to know what our main mission is. I need your word and word is bond. Do I have your word that this stays between us?"

The captains all said, "Yes, you have our word, but I thought our main mission was to destroy the demon queen and bring the kingdom back to God?"

Jehoiada said, "Yes, of course that is our main mission, but let me show you why it is our main mission."

Jehoiada then had Jehosheba to bring little Joash out for the captains to see and witness. Immediately the captain's eyes bucked and their mouths fell open. One captain said, "But, but I thought all of the Royal Family was dead, murdered by demon queen?"

Jehosheba said, "When all of the killing started I ran to Joash's room and grabbed him and his nurse and brought them here. He has been here with us for the last 6, almost 7 years."

All of the captains fell to the floor and bowed in reverence to Joash as King.

Jehoiada said, "Ok, here's the plan. After we have all of the weapons in place this is what will happen. When the guards change I want the guards that are leaving duty and the guards that are coming on duty to form a circle of protection around Joash our King. If anyone tries to break inside of that circle, my orders are to kill them on the spot right where they stand. King Joash is to be protected at all times. Seven years ago we all witnessed what that demon queen can do, so he must be protected at all times. Got it."

The captains nodded and said, "Yes, we will go and get things in order now, because in about an hour the guards will change and we want to do this as soon as possible. We are sick of that demon queen!"

The captains left and set everything in order. The orders were given and received. Everyone was on point and about getting that demon queen out of control.

When the guards changed, Jehoiada brought King Joash to the House of Worship and the guards formed a circle of protection around him.

Jehoiada said, "King Joash, I anoint you and with this crown, I crown you King of this land."

The guards and all the people in the land that were there clapped, applauded, screamed and chanted, "Long live the King! Long live the King!"

Jehoiada and the captains knew that this would bring the demon Queen Mother out into the open to see what was going on.

Upon hearing all of the noise and shouting Queen Mother was beside herself especially when she heard, 'Long live the King.' Queen Mother said, "What is going on with all that noise out there in them streets? What do they mean long live the King? Uh-uh! Naw, naw, don't they realize that I am the Queen

Mother and I am in control. Ain't no King runnin' nothin' round here! I took care of that seven years ago. Guards! Guards! Where in the world are the guards? In the name of Baal, guards!! I guess that I will need to go and check this out for myself. Ever since I killed everyone them guards been slackin' big time.'"

When Queen Mother finally arrived she looked around, frowned and scowled her ugly face and said, "What is going on here? Long live who? Oh no, ain't no long live the King. I don't know what y'all out here chantin' in these streets!"

Then she noticed Joash with a crown on his head and said, "Where did HE come from? He is supposed to be dead with all of the other members of the royal family that I ordered to be murdered. Which one of you guards missed this little rat! Why I will kill him myself. AND WHY is he wearing that crown? I am in charge of this kingdom. Take that crown offa him."

Queen Mother then lunged at King Joash and in that instant Jehoiada and the captains looked at each other and gave the bruh man nod. Time for the second part of the plan. The captain of the army let the demon queen say all that she had to say and then he said, "Demon, your time here is over! You no longer have a kingdom to rule and you certainly don't have a legal right or the authority to be here. We have grown sick and tired of your evil demonic ways. You treat us, the ones who protect you, like we are worthless and the main thing is that you have no respect for God himself!!"

The people said, "Yeah, that's right. Tell that ole wrinkled up witch to go somewhere and SAT down!! DOWN WITH THE QUEEN! DOWN WITH THE QUEEN!"

The captain continued, "You took the sacred worship items that are used to worship God and you started using them to worship your demon god Baal. How long did you think that we would take this? This is the 7th year and 7 is God's number for completion, so your time as Queen Mother over this land is done! King Joash is now in control and God is in control of him!"

Jehosheba spoke up and said, "Yeah sis. Ya know, I really, really tried hard to bring you back to the Lord our God and I told you time and time again that you were doing way too much and you needed to calm down and listen to God, but NAW, you just had to worship that demon god Baal and the more you worshipped him the worse you got. You were always stubborn and thought you knew it all, now look where it has gotten you. Your blood sacrifice to Baal failed. Joash is alive and the bloodline lives on!"

Jehoiada said, "Enough!! Guards PLEASE take her away and you know what to do!"

The captain said, "Be sure to take her outside of this sacred place of worship and if anyone tries to go with her and save her, kill them also. We don't need any straggling demons or imps left behind."

So the guards grabbed her old shriveled up body and took her over there where the horses were hanging out and slaughtered her like she was a Thanksgiving turkey.

Jehoiada the high priest said, "Let's pray! Father we thank you today for giving us the plan and the victory over evil. We declare this day that we are Your people, You are our God and we will have no other God but You! And Father I promise You that I will teach young King Joash Your ways according to the Scroll of God that I have given him. He will be a king that serves You and only You."

After Jehoiada finished praying the guards and the people of God went into the place of worship and destroyed everything that was used to worship Baal. They tore down the statue of Baal, the altar that Queen Mother used to worship Baal and they even killed the priest of Baal named Mattan. They didn't bother to take him to the horse stable, they killed him right in front of the altar!

One of the people was heard saying, "That's right priest Mattan, where yo god Baal at now? Yo boy ain't comin' is he?"

Another said, "Man his god Baal can't come save him cause he shattered all over the floor. Look there is a piece of his head over there!"

Everyone laughed and went straight for priest Matten to bring him to a bitter end!

After everything was all cleaned up and in place, King Joash was escorted to the throne in a royal parade. This was a glorious day and a special time to remember. King Joash was 7 years old when he became ruler of the land. He was so young that he didn't know a knife from a fork, but High Priest Jehoiada gave him the Scroll of God and taught him everything that he needed to know. As long as Jehoiada was alive Joash was a true and righteous King and did what was right in the eyes of God, but when High Priest Jehoiada died at 130 years of age and after all that he taught King Joash, Joash was persuaded to start worshipping the god of his murderous grandmother, Queen Mother Athialiah. Joash eventually grew into adulthood and had a son named Jeroboam who also worshipped Baal like his father and his murderous great grandmother Queen Mother Athialiah.

Jeroboam ruled for 41 years and his reign was known for greed, materialism, social wickedness and selfishness. They were all about getting the bag and anything else they wanted. No self-restraint what so ever.

During this 41 year reign of Jeroboam, God had His prophets to bring His word to the people of the land. One of those prophets was Prophet Hosea who was known as the "Prophet of Doom" for those that did not want to hear God's message, but for those that did want to hear the Word of God it meant hope and love.

Hosea's father's name was Beeri. This is not the same Beeri as Esau's Father-in-law in Genesis

26, Beeri the Hittite. This is a different man named Beeri and it is pronounced Be-air-ee.

Hosea is the first Minor Prophet mentioned in the Old Testament. Although he is called a Minor Prophet, he was just as powerful as the Major Prophets. Hosea had a lot of work to do because the time he lived in was incredibly evil. All of the craziness that Jeroboam's great grandmother the demonic Queen Mother did when she was alive increased with the crowning of each king in her bloodline. Her evil was passed down in the royal bloodline and with each king they seemed to increase the level of evil in the land. The Queen Mother shed blood, so there was a lot more bloodshed in the land while King Jeroboam ruled. Poor people couldn't catch a break! The Queen Mother thought that the average person was worthless to society and that attitude was even stronger with Jeroboam. Chile look-a-here, it was a hot bed of do what you want, to who you want and how you want to do it. It was just a seething bed of evilness!!

Hosea had just come out of a 5 day revival. God's people were still taking about how the spirit of God moved, healed, delivered and set people free. Hosea was at home resting and reflecting on how God had used him and all of a sudden God spoke to him and said, "Hosea."

Hosea said, "Yes God."

God said, "Ok, because of how you answered, I know that you know this is Me talking to you. I want you to go out there in the Red Light District and find the best looking street walkin' ho' that you can and marry her."

Hosea said, "The devil is a liar! How can I marry a street walkin' ho'? What would that do to my godly reputation? I am out here prophesying Your Word and, and telling people to live right and now I am supposed to go and marry a ho'?! That doesn't even sound right! I could maybe see if she were an escort who worked behind closed doors, but You said a street walkin' ho'! Are You messing with me right now God? It doesn't matter how pretty she is, her life is jacked up and quite frankly I have kept myself from being sexually active, saving myself for my righteous, holy and saved wife and guess what God, I don't want someone who has slept with and who has had sex with every man in town. The devil is a liar and the truth certainly ain't in him."

God said, "Now I established upfront that you knew whose voice this is. You know My voice when you are in revival and speak on My behalf.   You know who this is! I am not the devil and I ain't no liar. I am going to tell you this one more time and you had betta get yo crack up and go do as I say! I want you to go out there in them streets and find the best looking street walkin' ho' that you can and marry her. Got it!"

Hosea was like a little child at this point who had gotten caught eating cookies after being told no. Hosea said, "Yes, God I got it! But IOWN understand why I gotta do this! How come you didn't tell one of them Major Prophets to do it? Their spiritual reputation can take the hit. I'm just a Minor Prophet. This just ain't right."

Hosea even let a few tears fall and fell out on the floor until he heard God say, "Man I am NOT playin' with you. GET YO SELF UP offa that floor and go do what I said."

Hosea got up with a quickness!! He knew that God was about 5 seconds off that behind of his. God said, "Now that you have pulled yourself together here is the rest of your orders. I not only want you to find yourself the best looking street walkin' ho out there in them streets, and marry her, but as soon as you get married I want you two to get busy making some babies."

Hosea said, "Dang God, the whole nine huh?"

God said, "Yes, the whole nine and this is why, this kingdom that King Jeroboam rules over is nothing but a whore house and no longer is faithful to me their God. They run around and cheat on me with Baal and treat me like I don't exist. I want them to see a living example of how they look to me!"

Even though the man of God, Hosea, did not agree with his assignment he got up and headed

30

down to the Red Light District where all of the ho's hang out and he went to the busiest corner where the ho's pick up their marks.

The closer that Hosea got to the district the more nervous he became. Oh boy was sweatin' bullets and thinking, "This is not how I wanted to find a wife. I wanted a bae! Someone who is going to love me and love God. This ho' won't even know who God is!"

Hosea was now in the Red Light District. He was approached by all of the women on the corner cause he was a handsome man and was a regular gym rat and it showed. One of the women was heard to say, "Oh Lord, the Man of God is here! Did you come to preach a revival to us? You gotta a word from the Lord for us?"

Another one said, "Yeah, I know you didn't come down here for what I think you did! Word from the Lord my behind, he still a man!"

The main one named Gomer, the daughter of Diblaim said, "Y'all move outta the way. This is truly a Man of God, show some respect. Haven't y'all seen how those other supposed men of God move? He don't move like that at all.'"

Gomer continued speaking to Hosea, "What can I do for you? What brings YOU down here to these parts? You do know what happens here, right?"

Hosea said, "Yes, I am aware of how y'all pick up men, have sex and get paid. I am here for you!"

Gomer said, "For me? What could you possibly want with me? With all due respect I know the offerings from your little revivals are good and all, but believe me you cannot afford me! Believe me when I tell you, I am the best there is around here!"

Hosea said, "Look, God told me to come down here and find the best lookin' ho', I mean lady, and marry here. That happens to be you."

Gomer said, "Yeah right, God told you!"

The other ladies laughed and said, "Here we go! We have seen this before. God told him to come down here and find the best lookin' ho and marry her!! OMG! The lies they tell just to be with us."

Another one said, "Well, at least we know this man of God ain't married like the others that pull up on us!"

Then they all said, "Right, right. You sho right about that."

Hosea said, "Naw, it ain't like that! I am for real! I got the ring right here. 2.5 carats! Baby I ain't playin'! God ain't playin' with me and I gotta do what He said to do. So Gomer…"

Then Hosea got down on one knee and said, "So Gomer, will you PUH-LEASE marry me and become my wife and the mother of my children?"

Boy they were laughing now! One was rolling all over the ground laughing and saying, "GO-MER!! HEY GOMER!! Chile you got something right there! Whatcha gonna do, huh, whatcha gonna do?"

The others joined in and made it a song, "GO-MER will you marry me, will you marry me? Will you marry me! Whatcha gonna, whatcha gonna do, uh-huh, uh-huh whatcha, whatcha, whatcha gonna do!"

The street traffic and the people walking seemed to stop as Hosea was down there on one knee waiting for Gomer to answer him. Hosea started to feel a little faint as the anointing of God came over him and saturated that corner. Just as he started to get up and leave thinking that he had found the wrong lady, Gomer said, "What the heck. Why not? You are a handsome well-built man and I know that the man of God got some dollars, so yeah, why not!"

The others said, "Gurl NO! Don't be fooled. He probably gonna take you somewhere and tie you up and try to preach the sex demon out of you. We have all had that to happen."

Gomer said, "No, this is different. I feel something kind and sweet about him. I am all in."

Hosea was screamin', clappin' his hands and dancin' the sanctified holiness, done got my breakthrough, dance. Hosea said, "Yes! She said yes. Thank You God for sending me to the right one, the best one, the prettiest one."

Hosea and Gomer left the area and went straight to one of Hosea's pastor friend's house to get married. When they showed up on the pastor's doorstep and rang the bell Hosea began to feel ashamed and thought, "What is he going to say to me? I will be ruined. Lord!"

The pastor opened the door and said, "Hey man whazzup? What you doing here so late and who is that with you?"

Hosea said, "Hey man, I need a big favor?"

Pastor said, "Yeah?"

Hosea said, "I need you to marry us?"

Pastor said, "At this late hour? And is there something wrong that you can't wait and plan a proper wedding? I know she ain't pregnant, not the way that you was preaching and calling people out about sex before and outside of marriage! I just know that ain't the case, is it?"

Hosea said, "Look, may we come in?"

Pastor said, "Yeah, y'all come on in outta the dark and night air and outta the range of listening ears. Ya know people love ear hustlin' especially if the conversation is coming from my house."

Once they were inside in the light the pastor said, "OMG! Man I know who that is! That is Gomer, the biggest and prettiest ho' out there in the Red Light District! Whazzup with this? Man puh-leeze have a seat."

Hosea said, "Dude, God spoke to me right after the revival ended and told me to go find the prettiest street walkin' ho' in the Red Light District, marry her and have children with her."

Pastor said, "Naw man, you kidding me! Why in the world would God have a man of God like you to marry someone like that? No offense Gomer, but you two are from two different worlds."

By this time the pastor's wife had come downstairs and thought that she had better fix some coffee after what she overheard.

Hosea said, "Man listen, this is the reason God told me to do this, he said 'This kingdom that King Jeroboam rules over is nothing but a ho' house and is no longer faithful to Me, their God. They run around on Me with Baal and treat Me like I don't exist. I want them to see a living example of how they look to Me!'"

Pastor said, "Man say no more! I heard God say that same thing to me when I was in my prayer closet, just tonight. I know that this is really God. I am ready when you are ready and I see that my wifey has gotten up and she can be a witness."

Hosea said, "Man thank you for knowing me and knowing that I move when God says move and He has spoken."

Gomer was sitting there all of this time feeling a bit uncomfortable but listening and looking around and thinking to herself, "It will be nice to get off these streets. It certainly ain't as safe as it used to be, and with all of the church men that come through I might as well be in church! Mm…Pastor sure does have a beautiful house, I certainly hope that Hosea's house is as nice as this one. A girl could get used to this!"

Hosea looked at Gomer and said, "I know that we do not know each other at all, but just like God worked it out for you to say yes to marry me, He will make our marriage loving and blissful. Just trust me, He has got us."

Pastor said, "Yes, He has got you two. Are you ready to do this?"

And with that Hosea and Gomer were married and on their way to getting down to grown folks business. And of course when they did, Gomer got pregnant.

Chile, Gomer went back down to the Red Light District and handed out invitations to her old crew to come to the gender reveal party. And yes, they all showed up in full fabulous fashion mode. The weave was flyin', the fish net stockins' showed a rainbow of colors, and of course thighs and hips mixed with too much cleavage was showin'! Look-a-here, CHILE, the church folks didn't like that at all, they already felt some kind of way about Gomer being the Prophet's wife! Now this!

One was heard saying, "How in the world is she gone invite them to be HERE at the same time that WE are? Couldn't she have simply showed them the baby pictures after the baby is born? And what is that smell? What kinda cheap perfume is that? Why I never smelled anything like it. I just never!!"

Another one said, "I know that's right. The Bible does say that light should not have fellowship with darkness, that is pure darkness and I don't want any parts of it!"

Then you heard a bunch of, "Yeah. Uh huh. That part!! Don't nobody want to be dealing with all of that! HUH!!"

One of the other pastor's wife said, "Girl I was in church the first time that Prophet Hosea bought Gomer to church with him. You should have seen how the men were acting. They were showing off, trying to show Gomer who could sing the best and pray the hardest. It is ashamed that the most eligible and most God fearing man around married someone like that!

Then again you heard a bunch of, "Yeah. Uh huh. I was there and saw that too. These menzez is too much!! Don't nobody want to be dealing with all of that! They know that they need to sit down somewhere and stop tryna show off. God sees all of that! Yes, He does."

Gomer overheard what they were saying and lit right into them. She wasn't having that! Gomer said, "Don't give me that why I never routine, and quoting scripture to fit your stink attitude. Don't say why I never, cause yes you did!! Don't be up in here acting all holier than thou! All of y'all need to step back and shut it up! I saw many of your husbands down on the corner many times talkin' bout they got a Word from the Lord and needed to minister the word in private. I even heard word from the male escorts that a couple of you, supposed church-o-crits, holier than thou ladies, were at the local spot pushin' up all over them. Shoot some of you were seen with members of my crew, talkin' bout you are curious and want to know what it's like to be with a lady then you gone sit up here and quote scripture! If you want to quote a scripture, let's go there!! How about touch not, taste not! Oh that's right you already did that!!"

The crew was laughing so hard that one of them had to run to the bathroom. They were enjoying this tongue lashin'.

Gomer continued, "How about love thy neighbor! See y'all actin' like you straight up street, but let me tell you, you really don't want me to bring that kinda heat. Oh No, you don't! And as far as your men in the church, if you would fix yourself up and stop lookin' so homely your men wouldn't be lookin' at me tryna show off and I see y'all lookin' at my man when you already have a whole man! You betta get right, you betta get right! Keep it one hundred ladies, cause we already know the deal! Keep it a buck and stop runnin' after BUCK! Stop the drama, shut up or leave."

GURL, the other church folk gasped, fanned their white hankies and held their chests. Chile the crew was enjoying themselves while Gomer was lightin' them church-o-crits up! The crew went in the back where the food was to talk amongst themselves and to feast on them bbq ribs, fried chicken and potato salad. Let's not mention the sweet potato pies, they didn't EVEN stand a chance.

One of the crew said to Gomer, "Thanks for comin' in here away from all of that!"

The rest of the crew said, "Yeah gurl. That was too much! You got your hands full on the real with them old biddies. They in there talkin' all that ra-ra stuff!"

They all looked at each other and said, "Anywhoo -Gurl!! Y'all gotta beautiful place! I love this furniture."

The rest of the crew said, "YASS. We know who got the money. Maybe we in the wrong profession!"

They all laughed and continued to look around and enjoy themselves.

It was time for the reveal and guess what, it was all blue!!! Hosea and Gomer were having a boy!! God spoke to Hosea and said, "You will name him Jezreel."

Hosea whispered the name in Gomer's ear and Gomer said, "God said it and his name will be Jezreel."

Gomer then told her crew what the baby's name would be. Now we know that the crew didn't understand spiritual things. You would think that they would have a little understanding of where Gomer was since marrying Hosea, left the street life and settled down. But NAW! One of them said, "Gurl, you gonna name that baby Jezreel? What kinda name is that for a baby? Sounds like an old man's name or some rapper tryna come up with a new hook."

Another one said, "Yeah, it sounds like something, don't know what yet, but something. Why can't you just name the baby boy Jayquan or Raheem, ya know somethin' NORMAL!!"

Gomer said, "Look, God said to name him Jezreel."

Hosea said, "Yeah because the time is coming and very soon when God is going to bring the pay back to Israel for how they massacred the people of Jezreel."

Then Hosea began to prophesy as the spirit of God fell in their home and automatically the church-o-crits hands went up in the air, their eyes were closed and they started speaking in tongues. Hosea continued, "God said He is too through with the kingdom of Israel. It's time for the payback! He said that He is going to burn up Israel's weapons at the Valley of JEZREEL as it burns."

Then Hosea looked at Gomer and said, "Honey God said that our son Jezreel will be full of His fire, power and anointing."

Chile revival was on and poppin' at the gender reveal party. The church-o-crits started going way in. The crew looked at Gomer and said, "Gurl, we out! Nice party and all, good food and good to see you, but er-um we didn't come here for no church service or revival as y'all call it. We out!"

As they walked out the front door they all felt the power of God, but were too stubborn to stay and receive the fullness of His power to change.

After it was all over Gomer looked at Hosea and said, "Honey that was really nice. I never had a real party of any kind in my entire life."

She started to cry and Hosea held her and said, "Aww baby. You deserve it."

Well, it wasn't long before Gomer was pregnant again. That chile was extremely fertile! Gurl-friend started having babies like there was no tomorrow. She got pregnant again and this time she had a girl and God told Hosea, "Name the baby-girl No-Mercy."

Hosea said to God, "What kinda name is that for my baby girl. Mercy is a pretty name, but No-Mercy?"

God said, "No-Mercy is the baby's name because I have had it with Israel. I have given them times and periods of mercy after mercy and now I have no more mercy to give them and no more forgiveness for them. At least I didn't say name the baby No-Forgiveness. Now that would have been an odd mess!"

Hosea said, "Yeah, you are certainly right. No-Forgiveness would have been bad. Gomer probably would have killed me."

God said, "Don't you worry about Gomer. Just remember this, I have no more mercy for Israel, but I will continue to show mercy towards Judah. I will be the God of Judah that saves them. They think that they have power but their armies and weapons of warfare will not save them, I will."

Hosea had a night service and that was the message for that night, "God said No-Mercy."

That was a powerful message and many gave their lives to the Lord. The morning ride radio show gave all the details of who got saved, who fell out on the floor and how much weave they collected at the end. The D.J. even put a price on the weave and gave the type and color.

It wasn't but about nine months later that Gomer became pregnant again. I am beginning to wonder if the Prophet Hosea did anything else but be fruitful and multiply! Anywho, this time they had another boy and God told Hosea, "Name him "Nobody."

Hosea said, "God I ain't even gonna question you on this. The boy's name will be Nobody. Please protect him as he goes to school because he will be ruthlessly teased by the other children."

God said, "The boy will be alright. I have My protection on his life. The reason that I want him named Nobody is because this land has become a nobody to Me and I have become a nobody to them."

My God that word hit Hosea like a sword in his heart and that night at service he preached that word like tomorrow was cancelled and life was over.

The next day Gomer took her children down to the Red Light District to see the crew and she told them, "This is my oldest son Jezreel. Y'all remember we had the gender reveal party for him and you all were there? Well this is him, isn't he beautiful? And this is my daughter No-Mercy and my youngest son Nobody."

The crew went into overdrive. Chile they started laughing and falling out. Gomer took off her earrings and shoes and said, "Why y'all laughing at my babies?"

One of them finally spoke and said, "We ain't laughing AT your babies, they are beautiful, but where in the world did you come up with those names? That's what we laughin' at!"

Then they all said, "Wait, wait, don't tell us, GOD TOLD YOU!"

One of the crew said, "Gurl! You named your baby boy Jezreel that's bad enough, but then you named your baby GURL NO-MERCY! Either that's gonna scare every man away from her or she will have men flocking at her feet."

Another one chimed in and said, "YASS, YASS. That poor baby! We all know just how cruel kids can be. Hopefully she will have NO MERCY on them when she lightin' they butts up for pickin' at her! You are going to teach them how to protect themselves, right?"

Then they all looked at each other and sang, "NOBODY!! NOBODY!!"

One of the crew said, "Chile, that boy gone have low self-esteem, low self-worth, and low everything! He's gonna feel like a ghost, like he doesn't exist and he will certainly feel like someone that NOBODY sees. How could you do that to him?"

Gomer got straight serious and said, "YES, GOD TOLD ME and MY MAN how to name our children. You had betta stop all that laughin' and recognize who you talkin' to and about! You wouldn't understand anyways! Now I see what the church folk meant about y'all."

One of the crew said, "Oh no she didn't!"

Another said, "Oh yes she did. She went straight there!"

Gomer grabbed up here earrings, shoes and her children and left like it was a fire in an old dried up shack.

Meanwhile God was still speaking to Hosea and saying, "Hosea, in just a little while there will be so many Israelites that you won't be able to count them with the stars. They will be like sand blowing all over the place and they will no longer be nobodies, but everybody will recognize them as somebody! Not only that, but Israel and Judah will come together as one and they will no longer have two separate leaders, but one leader will rule over them both. They will be a mighty force to be reckoned with. They will be powerful and that will be a great day in Jezreel!"

When Gomer finally came home she came in hot!! She was still mad with the crew for all that they had to say about her baby's names. She flung the door open and when the children were settled she told Hosea, "You just wouldn't believe what I just had to put up with from my own crew!"

Hosea said, "Whassa matter baby? Who done upset my honey?"

Gomer said, "Alright with the baby talk. I'm too mad right now for the baby talk. Why did God have to name my babies those weird and hot mess names? Our poor children will be picked at all of their lives, especially No-Mercy. And Nobody will never stand a chance. He won't be able to live out his full potential because his self-worth and self-esteem will be so low due to his name. He won't even believe in himself!"

Hosea said, "Aww honeeeyy! It won't be like that. Our daughter will be feared by all and only those that have a good heart and mean her no harm will be able to ride with her. She will have no mercy on those that try to bully her or her brothers. She will be a leader and have many followers. We will make sure that all of our children take and master martial arts so that they can physically defend themselves

56

and more importantly we will be sure that they know how to walk in the power and authority that God gave them so that they can spiritually defend themselves. As far as Jezreel and Nobody, their names will be famous! I see it now. They will be famous musicians for the kingdom of God. Jez-reel or Just-real and Nobody or NB-Dee-Y will not only be prophetic musicians and prophetic rappers, but they will write music and lyrics and executively produce many groups, in many genres of music. So our children will be just fine baby. Don't listen to the haters, they don't know what's up!"

Hosea embraced and held Gomer and afterwards they settled down for a nice family dinner and a family game night of, "What's the Word." Yes, they were training their children at an early age how to hear God's voice, know His voice and release His Word.

Sometimes you just gotta shut the haters and the outside noise outta your world and live YOUR life!!

Point (s) to Ponder: Was God's purpose met when He named the babies? Why did Gomer continue to keep the people from her past in her life and bring them into the lives of her new family? Should she have let go of her past and move forward in all newness?

Take Away: Sometimes and most times when God moves you up and out of old situations and is doing a new thing in your life, everybody can't make that move with you. All energy ain't the right energy. When God moves, you must get on the frequency that He is transmitting to you and YOU stay there until He moves you again.

Prayer: Father we thank You today for how You are moving in our lives and we ask that You would give us the strength and ability to walk away from the past as You move us forward, into our divine destiny with You.